P9-CRO-106

A VISIT TO THE
United Kingdom

REVISED AND UPDATED

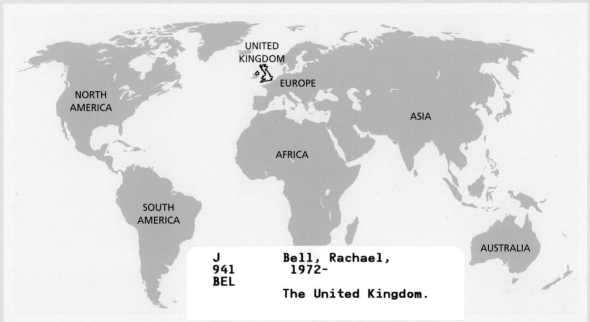

Rachael Bell

Heinemann Library
Chicago, Illinois

©2008 Heinemann Library
a division of Pearson, Ltd.
Chicago, Illinois

Customer Service 888-454-2279

Visit our website at www.heinemannlibrary.com

Designed by Heinemann Library
Printed in the United States, North Mankato, MN

12 11 10
10 9 8 7 6 5 4 3 2

Library of Congress Cataloging-in-Publication Data
Bell, Rachael, 1972-
The United Kingdom / Rachael Bell
p. cm
 Includes biographical references and index.
 Summary: Introduces the land, landmarks, homes, food, clothing, work, transportation, language, and culture of the United Kingdom.
ISBN: 978-1-4329-1274-1 (lib.bdg.), ISBN 978-1-4329-1293-2 (pbk.)
1. Great Britain--Juvenile literature. 2. Ireland --Juvenile literature. [1. Great Britain. 2. Ireland] I. Title. II. Series
DA27.5.B45 1999
941--dc21 98-45091

Acknowledgements
The publishers would like to thank the following for permission to reproduce photographs: © Ace Photo Agency p. **8** (Geoff Smith); © Alamy pp. **10** (Alan Copson City Pictures), **12** (Dave Pattison), **14** (Adrian Sherratt), **25** (Jeff Morgan Education); © Anthony Blake Photo Library p. **13** (Gerrit Buntrock); © Aviemore Photographic p. **27**; © Collections p. **6** (Gena Davies); © Corbis p. **11** (Arcaid/Charlotte Wood); © Images Color Library pp. **5**, **7**; © J. Allan Cash Ltd pp. **15**, **17**, **19**, **21**, **22**, **23**, **24**, **26**, **29**; © Link p. **16** (Orde Eliason); © Shakespeare's Globe p. **28**; © Tony Stone Images p. **20** (Penny Tweedie); © Trip pp. **9** (P. Rauter), **18** (C. Kapolka).

Cover photograph reproduced with permission of © Lonely Planet Images/Anders Blomqvist.

Our thanks to Nick Lapthorn for his comments in the preparation of this book.

Every effort has been made to contact copyright holders of any material reproduced in this book. Any omissions will be rectified in subsequent printings if notice is given to the publishers.

082010
005838RP

Contents

Any words appearing in bold, **like this**, are explained in the Glossary.

The United Kingdom

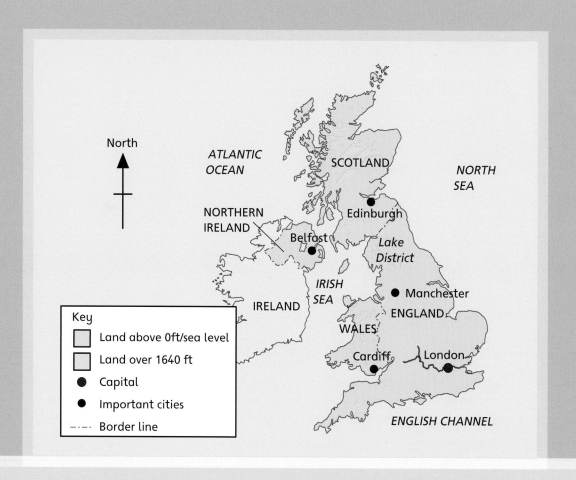

North

ATLANTIC OCEAN

SCOTLAND

NORTH SEA

NORTHERN IRELAND

Edinburgh

Belfast

Lake District

IRISH SEA

IRELAND

Manchester

ENGLAND

WALES

Cardiff

London

Key

- Land above 0ft/sea level
- Land over 1640 ft
- ● Capital
- ● Important cities
- --- Border line

ENGLISH CHANNEL

The United Kingdom is made up of a large island called **Great Britain**, part of Ireland, and lots of little islands.

People call the United Kingdom "the UK," for short. There are four different areas in the UK that used to be separate countries. These are England, Northern Ireland, Scotland, and Wales.

There are small villages in the UK as well as big cities.

Land

The north of **Great Britain** has mountains and deep valleys and lakes. In the south, there are gentle hills with wide rivers, where it is easier to grow crops.

There is lots of rain on the high land in the west of the country. Rain makes the grass and plants grow well there.

There are deep and wide valleys in Wales.

Landmarks

The Giant's Causeway in Northern Ireland is a strange **volcanic** rock on the coast. **Legend** says it was a giant's road that was built to step over the sea into Scotland.

The Tower of London was once a prison castle.

London, the **capital** of the UK, has many famous buildings. Many **tourists** go to see the **keepers** and the **crown jewels** at the Tower of London.

Homes

Most people in the UK live in houses in towns or cities. Many of these houses were built over 100 years ago.

Some people live in blocks of apartments. New ones are being built and some empty old buildings in city centers are being made into apartments.

These apartments are in the east of London.

Food

You will find a fish and chip shop in every town. Because the UK is an island, fishermen supply fresh fish throughout the year. Chips, or french fries, are a popular snack.

Different parts of the UK have their own special dishes but many families enjoy a **traditional** Sunday lunch. This is usually a big piece of cooked meat, which is eaten with potatoes, other vegetables, and **gravy**.

Clothes

Many famous **fashion designers** come from the UK. Young people enjoy wearing modern, fashionable clothes. Sports clothes are also very popular.

There are hundreds of different tartan patterns.

One of the **traditional** types of clothes in the UK is the **tartan** kilt. This is a checked, wool skirt worn by Scottish men and women on special occasions.

Work

Eight out of ten people in the UK work in a service industry. This means that they work in transportation, **education**, health and leisure, or money-related work.

Most other people work in industry. This means that they help to make or build things such as cars. Very few people work in farming in the UK.

Transportation

The London Underground was opened over 100 years ago. It used **steam trains** at first. Now it uses electricity. Three million people travel on it every day.

People drive on the left side of the road in the UK.

Most people travel to work by car and goods are transported by truck. This means that the roads and highways are very busy and there is a lot of **pollution**.

Language

Almost everybody in the UK speaks English. Each area has a different **accent**. Sometimes it can be hard for people from different areas to understand each other.

Street signs in Wales are in both Welsh and English.

In the UK about 750 thousand people speak Welsh and some people speak **Gaelic**. Some people speak other languages because their parents or grandparents came from other countries.

School

Children have to go to school from the age of 5 until they are 16. They study science, geography, history, English, music, math, art, and physical education.

In some schools students wear a jacket called a blazer.

Most schools are free and children from the local area go there. Some schools charge parents money and sometimes the children live there during the school terms.

Free Time

Many famous sports, such as soccer, tennis, and cricket, have come from the UK. Children play these both in and out of school. Adults also play these sports in their free time.

Many people enjoy being outdoors.
Some go to the beach in summer.
Others go walking or ride bicycles in the
mountains in the Lake District or Scotland.

These people are enjoying being outdoors in Wales.

Celebrations

The biggest celebration of the whole year is Christmas. The streets are lit with Christmas lights. People buy presents for each other and eat special Christmas food.

Burns Night is on January 25 every year.

Another special celebration in Scotland is Burns Night. People wear **tartan** clothes, and eat a special food called haggis. They listen to **bagpipe** music.

The Arts

The UK is famous for its theater. The plays of **Shakespeare** are very well known all around the world. Also, there are many theaters and theater festivals.

Wales is famous for its **male voice choirs**.

The UK has many musicians and pop groups. In Wales the Eisteddfod festival is a big competition for people who sing, write poetry, or play music.

Fact File

Name   The full name of the UK is the United Kingdom of **Great Britain** and Northern Ireland.

Capital   The **capital** city of the UK is London.

Language   Most people speak English, but some also speak Welsh or Gaelic.

Population There are about 60 million people living in the United Kingdom.

Money   Money in the UK is the pound (£), which is divided into 100 pence. Scotland and Wales also have their own coins and bank notes.

Religions There are many Christians in the UK, as well as Muslims, Sikhs, Hindus, Jews, and Buddhists.

Products   The UK produces oil and gas, wheat and other foods, chemicals, cars, and other transportation machinery.

Welsh Gaelic words you can learn

diolch (DEE-olkh)	thank you
bore da (boh-re-DAR)	good morning
nos da (norse-dar)	good night
hwyl fawr (hooeel-vowr)	goodbye
ie (EE-eh)/na (nar)	yes/no

Glossary

accent a different way of saying the same word

bagpipes a musical instrument that you blow. It has pipes and a bag to collect the air

capital the city where the government is based

crops the plants that farmers grow and harvest (gather)

crown jewels the crowns and special jewels worn by the Queen of Great Britain

education anything to do with teaching children or adults

fashion designers people who draw ideas for clothes which are then made

Gaelic the ancient language of the people who first lived in Scotland, Ireland, Wales, and Breton in France

gravy meat juices that are made into a sauce

Great Britain an large island in Europe where England, Scotland, and Wales are

keepers people who wear special clothes and protect a building

legend a well-known, old story

male voice choir group of men who get together to sing

pollution dirt and poisons that fill the air, usually made by car and truck engines

Shakespeare a man who lived over 400 years ago. He wrote plays and poems that are still popular today.

steam train an old type of train that burned coal to make steam which made the engine work

tartan woollen cloth with a check pattern in different colors

tourist person who is travelling to other places for holidays or to see the sights

traditional the way things have been done or made for a long time

volcanic a type of rock that has melted and is pushed out from beneath the Earth's surface

Index